Cryptocurrency

A Comprehensive And Accessible Guide For Novice
Individuals Seeking To Comprehend And Profit From The
Realm Of Cryptocurrency Trading, Non-Fungible Tokens
The Metaverse, And Decentralized Finance

Herfried Rohrmoser

TABLE OF CONTENT

Cryptocurrency - What Is It?

Cryptocurrency is a form of digital currency that is safeguarded through the implementation of cryptographic techniques. These monetary units do not have a physical counterpart and exist solely within the digital realm.

On October 31, 2008, Satoshi Nakamoto introduced the notion of a completely decentralized digital currency system in the article titled "Bitcoin: a peer-to-peer e-cash system" within the cryptography mailing list. In spite of various conjectures, the true identity of the individual or collective responsible for this pseudonym remains undisclosed.

In the initial stages of 2009, Satoshi Nakamoto introduced the inaugural iteration of the Bitcoin wallet and inaugurated the Bitcoin network. The digital currency exhibits various notable benefits.

Firstly, inflation does not have overwhelmingly negative consequences. In the event that the printing press experiences a malfunction and generates a substantial quantity of paper currency, it follows logically that this currency would undergo a depreciation in value. With bitcoins, this scenario is effectively mitigated as the bitcoin code implements a strict constraint on the mining of only 21 million bitcoins.

Another plus is decentralization. The system lacks a singular central authority for management, thereby rendering it inherently resilient to attempts to forcefully curtail the circulation of currency and disrupt its operation. The network lacks a singular proprietor and instead is governed collectively by users spanning across the globe.

An additional benefit lies in the preservation of anonymity. It is possible to monitor transactions and ascertain the movement of bitcoins between wallets; however, it is considerably challenging to ascertain the precise individual who legitimately owns a given wallet. Any individual has the ability to initiate the process of establishing a Bitcoin account. This necessitates the utilization of suitable software and access to the Internet.

One of the most astonishing aspects is the fact that currency that does not exist in the physical realm possesses the ability to procure goods and services. However, it is undeniable that it possesses the capability to be utilized as a medium of exchange for commodities and services in a manner akin to physical currency notes or coins found within one's personal possession.

Cryptocurrencies have the capability to be converted into euros or dollars, as per your discretion. In numerous nations, individuals engage in the purchase of real estate, tickets, and gadgets using bitcoins as a form of payment. Additionally, bitcoins are also utilized for the payment of utility bills and the purchase of coffee, with even prominent entities like Microsoft accepting this digital currency.

In the year 2013, an intriguing incident occurred where a participant of a forum focused on bitcoins expressed a willingness to trade 10,000 bitcoins in return for a pair of pizzas. A different user concurred, proceeded to purchase a pizza, and presented him with bitcoins for a digital wallet. Therefore, the initial user purchased a pair of pizzas for the sum of 10,000 bitcoin, a certain amount of the digital currency which currently holds a value exceeding $21 million.

In the United States, due to challenges related to ascertaining the legal classification of cryptocurrency, conducting transactions involving the exchange of bitcoins for goods or services becomes more intricate. Consequently, it is advisable to primarily regard cryptocurrency as an investment alternative. Currently, the game is undeniably worthwhile as the value of bitcoin continues to steadily increase. Opt for either the possibility of significant financial gains or a sense of absolute security, as the most lucrative investments invariably coincide with the most pronounced risks.

2. What is Bitcoin?
Bitcoin is «digital cash». This serves the dual function of functioning as a digital

currency as well as an online payment system. Within this framework, the utilization of data encryption methodologies facilitates oversight of the production of currency units and verification of financial transactions. The system operates autonomously from the state central banks.

Bitcoin is recognized as the foremost and most extensive decentralized digital currency. Alternative cryptocurrencies, numbering less than one hundred, are commonly referred to as altcoins. However, it was the bitcoin that ultimately emerged as the prevailing standard, boasting the highest market capitalization.

Bitcoins are generated as an incentive for executing mathematical computations. The act of generating fresh blocks is referred to as mining.

Individuals contribute their computational resources to authenticate addresses and document transactions within the registry, in return for which they receive a commission for each transaction along with newly generated bitcoins.

Initially, the creation of blocks was comparatively effortless, and it was solitary miners who undertook this task. Over the course of time, the level of intricacy escalated due to the necessity for significant computational capabilities in mining. Consequently, the miners commenced collaborating in pools, combining their computational resources to collectively extract fresh bitcoins.

It can be rather perplexing to navigate the terminology as the terms "bitcoin" and "block" possess the capability to encompass any of the three fundamental aspects of this concept: the foundational block-technology, the protocol and client responsible for facilitating transactions, and the tangible form of cryptocurrency (currency).

3. What is Blockchain?

A blockchain is a versatile and hierarchical technological framework created for the dependable recording of diverse assets. The bitcoin network is comprised of interconnected transaction blocks. Each successive block incorporates information from the preceding one, enabling the construction of a cohesive chain that encompasses all prior transactions, while preserving the anonymity of bitcoin owners.

The primary distinction and indisputable benefit lies in the fact that this registry is not centrally stored. All individuals utilizing this network are eligible for a complimentary registration. Digital records are consolidated into "blocks", which are subsequently interconnected through intricate mathematical algorithms, ensuring cryptographic and chronological linkage into a coherent "chain." Each block is linked to the preceding one and encompasses a collection of records. Additional blocks are consistently appended solely to the conclusion of the chain.

The cryptographic process, referred to as hashing, is executed by a diverse array of computers operating within a shared network. Should the calculations yield identical outcomes for each of them, a distinctive digital signature (signature) will be granted to the block. Once the registry has been updated and a new block has been formed, it becomes immutable and cannot be altered thereafter. Consequently, it is unattainable to counterfeit it. It is solely permissible to append new entries to it. It is imperative to acknowledge that simultaneous updates of the registry occur across all network-connected computers. The availability of the latest version of the registry ensures its transparency for all stakeholders.

Potentially, this technology encompasses all domains of economic activity without any exceptions and possesses a wide range of practical applications. Included in the list are finance, economics, and cash settlements, as well as the management of physical assets (such as real property, real estate, and cars) and intangible assets (such as voting rights, ideas, reputation, intentions, medical data, and personal information).

To finalize a standard transaction, it is necessary to seek the services of a legal practitioner or notary, remit the required fees, and patiently await the issuance of the pertinent documents. Smart contracts function in a manner akin to automated vending machines, wherein bitcoins are deposited into the system (specifically, the ledger), and upon completion, the contracted service, whether it be a driver's license or any other service enlisted, is delivered directly to the user's account under the custodianship of a third party.

Moreover, in contrast to conventional agreements, smart contracts possess not only provisions outlining the responsibilities and consequences of non-compliance for the involved parties but also have the capability to autonomously guarantee the complete execution of all contractual terms.

Smart contracts enable the facilitation of transactions involving monetary funds, property, shares, or other valuable assets, devoid of the need for intermediaries.

During a recent conference on blockchain technology held in Washington, Vitalik Buterin, a programmer of merely 23 years of age affiliated with the Ethereum project, elaborated on the concept of intelligent contracts. In this framework, the transfer of an asset or currency takes place within a program that actively tracks adherence to a predefined set of conditions.

At a certain juncture, this program verifies the adherence to the contractual obligations and procedurally ascertains whether the designated asset should be allocated to one party involved in the transaction or promptly reverted to another participant (potentially with additional intricacies in the conditions). Throughout this duration, the documentation remains stored and replicated within the decentralized registry, thereby guaranteeing its trustworthiness and preventing any party from altering the terms of the agreement.

As an illustration, a sophisticated thermoregulation system possesses the capability to transmit data pertaining to power consumption to a sophisticated electrical network. Upon consuming a specific quantity of electricity, an automatic process is initiated wherein the necessary units are telecommunicated from your account to that of the energy company. Consequently, the meter's operation and the subsequent billing process have been automated.

A medical practitioner or an individual seeking medical attention may effectively transfer their private key to a medical apparatus, such as a blood glucose monitoring device for instance. Subsequently, this device has the capability to autonomously document the patient's blood glucose readings in accordance with safety protocols, and subsequently facilitate data exchange with an insulin administration device that can automatically regulate this blood parameter to a standard level using the aforementioned data.

This approach can also be utilized to regulate the utilization of intellectual property by specifying the frequency with which a user is allowed to access, disseminate, or duplicate information. Additionally, it can be employed to establish voting systems that are safeguarded against fraudulent activities, facilitate the unrestricted dissemination of information, and offer numerous other functionalities.

By employing smart contracts, individuals can effectively operate in a multitude of domains, encompassing logistics, administration, legal affairs, and even electoral processes.

Selecting An Optimal Cryptocurrency Trading Approach Suited To Your Needs

There exist numerous methodologies for engaging in cryptocurrency trading. Certain types are more suitable for an individual's preferences, tolerances, and objectives than others.

Scalping, Day Trading, Swing Trading, Intraday Trading, Range Trading, Position Trading, and Investing encompass distinct trading methodologies.

Whilst there exist diverse approaches to categorizing trading types, I shall delineate them as follows: scalping, day trading, intra-day trading, range trading, swing trading, position trading, and investing.

Scalping endeavors to achieve rapid and immediate transactions, day trading endeavors to execute profitable trades within the trading day, range trading involves trading within the established trading range, intraday refers to a form of day trading that spans across multiple days, swing trading entails moving from one predetermined level to another (generally over days or weeks), and position trading involves conducting trades over an extended period of time.

These categories exhibit variations, however, the underlying concept is a progression spanning from the most rapid trading technique, known as scalping, to the most protracted trading approach, commonly referred to as investing.

Individuals can select a style that suits their preferences or combine and match different styles based on their attributes or goals. Regardless, it is advisable to tailor your strategies to align with your trading style. Various tactics are most effective with different time frames. Investors, who prioritize larger time frames, tend to be less concerned with smaller time frames, volatility, and technical support/resistance. They typically maintain their main position unleveraged. Conversely, scalpers may attempt to utilize leverage to anticipate support and resistance on a 5-minute chart.

The most effective approach to determining the styles that suit you most is through conducting experiments and assessing honestly the level of skill you possess and their impact on your emotional and logical well-being.

In essence, if a particular style is causing disorientation and a sense of imbalance, it is not suitable for your needs (likewise, if you consistently experience defeat, that style is also unsuitable for you).

To a certain extent, expediting your decision-making process and minimizing the depletion of your financial resources will lower the risk associated with each trade on paper; however, it will necessitate a more hands-on approach to your trading activities. Furthermore, due to the frequent nature of your transfers, there is a likelihood of heightened confusion and the need for increased attention towards slippage and associated fees.

Based on the information provided, it can be deduced that position trading and investing present the most favorable alternatives for novice or occasional traders, as they entail reduced levels of constant monitoring and specialized knowledge. Nevertheless, within the realm of cryptocurrency, individuals engaged in trading and investment encounter supplementary pressures... due to the inherent volatility of the market, even over extended intervals.

In the interim, it is worth noting that engaging in trading strategies that necessitate holding positions overnight may induce mental strain, given that the cryptocurrency market operates continuously, spanning across all time zones, every day of the week. It is not unprecedented for price adjustments to take place during periods of sleep.

However, for individuals who may have reservations, engaging in role trading or investing, supplemented with the practice of dollar-cost averaging, would be a prudent initial step.

Please take note that the classifications presented on this page may be known as cryptocurrency investment modalities. Nevertheless, that is an entirely separate subject matter. Cryptocurrency trading can be conducted utilizing a diverse range of methodologies. In my perspective, investment approaches such as dollar-cost averaging, profit averaging, and similar strategies possess a greater appeal when it comes to establishing long-term positions in assets. The objective herein is to discuss trading strategies, which refer to methodologies for establishing positions with the aim of generating profit, as opposed to approaches for long-term asset investment (although some common ground exists, and investment concepts are also addressed).

VARIOUS APPROACHES TO CRYPTOCURRENCY TRADING

Now that we have addressed that matter, presented below are several thought-provoking illustrations of trading styles (applicable to all types of trading, although they will be elucidated specifically in relation to cryptocurrency):

Scalping

Scalping involves the execution of rapid trades with great speed and efficiency. The objective is to sustain a consistent stream of profitability, even if the magnitude of the profits is minimal. Profits will be effortlessly acquired, and expenditures will be swiftly reduced. One could engage in frequent trading, with intervals of just a few minutes between each trade, or alternatively, one could opt to scalp a few select opportunities during the course of a day. You are in search of advantageous trade opportunities, rather than just pursuing any trade. You should possess the capability to engage in both long and short positions (and, as a result, would need to partake in margin trading, even with a leverage of 1x, to facilitate short selling). You can, however, scalp by buying and selling on the spot (buying and selling crypto).

This document may necessitate the acquisition of Ether at a price of $700, subsequent selling at $705, followed by an acquisition at $702 and final sale at $710. In such circumstances, it may be advisable to establish a nearby termination point at a value of $698. Additionally, it may be advisable to establish a guideline wherein, in the event of a trade turning unfavorable, you are required to execute a gradual reduction of your spot position through manual means. You should seldom allow your positions to run freely; instead, it is imperative to establish profit objectives.

This necessitates constant concentration. However, if you possess the necessary expertise, you have the potential to earn a substantial income at a rapid pace.

This necessitates the presence of effective risk management techniques and a significant reliance on either luck or talent. However, in theory, it is possible to consistently achieve marginal gains, which can quickly accumulate into substantial advancements.

Suggestion: Conduct thorough investigation regarding risk-reward analysis in trading to aid you in determining optimal levels for setting stop orders. If you engage in scalping, it would be advisable to implement stop orders.

Day Trading

Day trading is akin to scalping, albeit with the distinction that trades are executed on a daily basis instead of every few minutes.

In a single day, a day trader has the option to engage in scalping, trading within a specific range, or even executing short-term position trades. They engage in day trading as they do not maintain their positions beyond a single trading day.

You continue to employ stop losses to strategically enter and exit positions, yet you pursue a higher degree of profit per transaction compared to a scalper. Additionally, you exhibit a greater inclination to tolerate ambiguity and allow certain positions to soar.

Please be aware that scalping is categorized as a type of day trading. However, for the sake of clarity, I will discuss them as distinct practices due to their distinct implications.

Range Trading

Cryptocurrencies have the ability to consistently establish a range of trading. The aforementioned choice would probably entail a type of consolidation, either through accumulation, where prominent participants amass more coins in preparation for the anticipated market upswing, or through distribution, wherein they sell coins at a high price before purposefully letting the market decline.

A range trader operates by trading within the established range and strategically placing stop orders. They exhibit indifference towards trading at the highest or lowest points of the range, as their objective is solely to purchase the lower boundary of the range with the assistance of a stop order, and subsequently sell at the upper boundary or gradually reduce their position towards the upper limits of the range.

Engaging in trading is logical due to the diverse range of options, leading to robust levels of support and resistance. You prioritize the pursuit of profitable and stable transactions within the existing range, while contrasting approaches favor trading the emergence of market trends or declines.

This could pertain to either day trading or intraday trading, with the objective being to conduct trades based on the range rather than purchasing during an upward trend or selling following a downward trend.

Intraday Trading

This pertains to a variant of day trading wherein positions can be retained for longer than a single day. It is as straightforward as that. Professional traders engage in this activity frequently, and there is no justification for them not being skilled at it. Given that the cryptocurrency market operates continuously without any downtime, the concept of a traditional trading day doesn't exist (the closest approximation being the daily conclusion of candlestick patterns). The automation of positions using software obviates the necessity to prematurely liquidate a short-term position based solely on the occurrence of a specific time, such as 4 p.m.

Swing Trading

The essence of swing trading lies in identifying levels of support and resistance, or in a broader sense, strategically determining entry and exit points, and maintaining the position until the target is achieved or other exit criteria are fulfilled.

In this context, one can express the same idea in a more formal tone: "In this strategy, you would enter the market at what you perceive to be the lowest point in the local market, also referred to as the support level, and then maintain your position until what you perceive to be the highest point in the local market, known as the resistance level. Throughout this process, you would gradually scale out of your position to secure profits." Engaging in a short position represents a contrary approach where one seeks to reduce their position from the highest point of the developing pattern to the lowest.

Swing trading is a trading strategy characterized by holding positions for several days or weeks. Therefore, you will have the opportunity to securely occupy a chair, rest upon it, observe its rhythmic undulations, and engage in similar activities without experiencing distress.

Focusing on swing trading could prove to be highly logical if one possesses a comprehensive understanding of technical analysis. Specifically, if an individual demonstrates the ability to assess market trends and identify potential support and resistance levels, this approach becomes all the more viable.

Swing trading entails capitalizing on the cyclical nature of cryptocurrency, strategically timing one's entry at the trough of the wave and skillfully navigating the upward trajectory as it oscillates, exemplified by long positions (as opposed to short positions).

The duration of time required is contingent upon the timeline depicted in the chart and the specific pattern being examined, yet typically, a movement of considerable length is expected.

Proficient swing traders adept at employing long and short positions in their trading endeavors achieve remarkable success with minimal effort expended. However, demonstrating an understanding of the pattern, maintaining composure, and relinquishing opportunities for intermediate rest require significant courage.

Please take note that, in my opinion, swing trading exhibits the utmost adaptability as a trading style and is relatively straightforward to become proficient in. This is primarily due to the fact that support and resistance levels on higher time frames have a tendency to exhibit stronger adherence compared to those on lower time frames. There is no compulsion for you to promptly acknowledge trade requests. Moreover,

Swing provides the opportunity to capture remarkable sequences of events. If you have an interest in engaging in trading, begin your journey at this point; in case you prefer investing over trading but still wish to reap advantages, consider exploring the option of role trading.

Position Trading

Position trading can be likened to an amplified version of swing trading or an investment-oriented approach to trading. You will endeavor to establish a durable long position at a low point or a short position at a high point, which you will subsequently maintain for extended periods ranging from weeks to months, or possibly even years.

This represents the most fundamental approach to trading, however, it requires a significant level of self-control and adherence to established principles. Let us contemplate an individual who has maintained a long position on

Bitcoin since its value was $5k, and simultaneously adopted a short position when it reached $12k (With the current price of BTC standing at $8.3k). Bitcoin experienced a significant surge, ascending from a starting point of $20,000 to a peak of $5,000, and subsequently reaching a pinnacle of $11,000. A disciplined position trader might have observed any of those activities, possibly adjusting their positions by partially reducing or reopening them, or perhaps completely exiting their positions when the trend became unfavorable following a significant drawdown from the peak.

Position trading can be likened to investment in the sense that it entails maintaining positions for an extended duration. However, it diverges from traditional investment strategies, as its ultimate objective is to achieve success through executing advantageous longer-term trades rooted in comprehensive market trends.

In the domain of cryptocurrency, it is imperative to exhibit determination in the face of turbulent fluctuations, endure the unpredictable trends of both bullish and bearish markets, navigate through favorable and unfavorable information, while maintaining unwavering focus on the ultimate objective.

Suggestion: It is advisable to integrate position trading with high-frequency trend signals, exemplified by the utilization of 50 and 200 days moving average crossovers. While the aforementioned approach is just a basic illustration, it is recommended to explore more sophisticated strategies. Upon the occurrence of a bearish cross, it is advisable to close a position and subsequently reestablish it when a bullish cross materializes. This approach is most effective when applied to trending assets, such as the prominent cryptocurrencies.

Investing

In my perspective, there exists a distinction between investing and selling. The fundamental nature of trading revolves around the occurrence and endeavor to achieve advantageous outcomes. Investment involves acquiring a tangible or intangible asset that acts as a means of preserving and enhancing its value as time progresses.

Warren Buffet is an individual engaged in entrepreneurial activities and financial investments. Purchasing shares instills in him a sense of acquiring a stake in the enterprise. If one possesses a Fortune 500 company, it is not preferable to realize income as its value increases; rather, one would strive for further expansion. A low price indicates a company with a reduced cost structure, a factor that seldom concerns traders.

Investors are more inclined to divest their shares if they are dissatisfied with the trajectory of the asset's price, as opposed to their dissatisfaction with its present dollar value.

Investors may not consistently employ stop loss strategies. Alternatively, they will assume a position within the asset and maintain it as long as the underlying rationale for its acquisition remains sound.

If you embody the true essence of a HODLer, there would be no necessity for you to regularly monitor rates or charts, unless you are seeking to augment your position at an opportune valuation.

Although investing and trading are distinct practices, there inevitably comes a juncture where purchases and sales must be executed. It is imperative to acknowledge that this approach holds appeal for certain individuals.

Please be advised that you have the option to fully commit to either of the aforementioned options or gradually transition into them. Certain individuals may employ accumulation algorithms to make numerous small transactions throughout the day, while others may gradually reach a desired position through incremental purchases. Additionally, some individuals might opt for a concentrated approach by going all-in on a single significant transaction. The particular style you select is inconsequential as long as it is congruous with your personality and is accompanied by a well-developed risk management strategy.

Suggestion: It is imperative to exercise patience when dealing with any of the aforementioned categories. It is not uncommon to observe a consecutive sequence of losses in day trading, or to witness a declining trend shortly after initiating a thoroughly researched long position (or an increasing trend after initiating a short position). It is a common occurrence for things to go awry. In order to determine whether a particular style is consistently effective, one must endure through its setbacks and avoid making judgments or applying it based solely on a few outcomes observed within a limited timeframe. The objective is to achieve a higher rate of correctness compared to incorrectness, rather than striving for infallible correctness at all times. It will require a substantial amount of time and effort to enhance your personal style, and adapting your strategies to suit the prevailing market conditions and specific cryptocurrencies being targeted will likely be necessary.

Why Blockchain Is Significant?

Blockchain serves as a decentralized digital ledger that chronicles all transactions involving cryptocurrencies. This technology has the potential to influence the way we conduct work and could indeed have significant implications for society as a whole. "Herein lie four rationales elucidating the significant nature of blockchain:

•Blockchain is secure

•Blockchain is straightforward

•Blockchain is sealed

• The utilization of blockchain technology enables the execution of decentralized transactions, free from reliance on a centralized authority or external entities such as banks.

The rapid progress of Blockchain technology suggests that there is no sign of a slowdown. In recent years, a multitude of previously deemed improbable occurrences have proven to be unfounded, such as exorbitant transaction costs, duplication of transactions, online fraud, data recovery, and the like. Notwithstanding, this issue can be mitigated through the application of Blockchain technology.

What is Blockchain technology?

Blockchain originated in the year 1991 as a method of efficiently storing and retrieving digitized information. Blockchain represents a transparent ledger accessible to limited parties in real-time. One of its key benefits is that the recorded data is inherently resistant to alteration without the consensus of all parties involved. IBM has effectively managed to establish a correlation wherein each fresh record is transformed into a distinct block endowed with a unique hash value. Integrating the individual blocks to form a sequence of records establishes a blockchain. The digital currency known as Bitcoin makes use of blockchain technology.

The implementation of blockchain facilitates the verification and traceability of complex transactions necessitating scrutiny and identification. It has the capability to facilitate secure transactions, reduce consistency expenditures, and expedite information transfer processing. Blockchain technology has the potential to facilitate contract management and verify the origin of a product. It can also be employed in electoral platforms and the administration of official certifications and property ownership documents.

Please be advised that the data is maintained in a sequential order. Furthermore, once the data is documented, any modifications to it are rendered unfeasible.

What are the benefits of utilizing blockchain technology?

Below, we present an overview of the primary benefits that your business can expect to attain through the integration of Blockchain technology:

• Its permanent nature as a computerized public ledger ensures that once a transaction is recorded, it becomes immutable.

•The constant security of Blockchain can be attributed to its encryption feature.

• The transaction occurs instantaneously and seamlessly, as the record is automatically updated.

• Due to its decentralized nature, there is no need for any intermediary charges.

• Members undertake the task of verifying and validating the legality of a transaction.

Enhancing Trust in Government

According to a review conducted by the Seat Exploration Centre in May of last year, it was stated that the level of trust the American public has in their government is approaching an unprecedented minimum. Approximately 25% of American citizens express their belief in the competence of the government in Washington to consistently make well-informed decisions, with 2% stating that they can trust the government "broadly speaking" and 22% asserting that they can trust them "most of the time." Only 18% of the American population express confidence in the ability of the government to consistently make sound decisions.

The consulting firm, Booz Allen Hamilton, contends that the government stands to gain significant advantages through the utilization of blockchain-based applications, as they inherently promote transparency through decentralization, thereby enabling all involved stakeholders to access and validate data. Likewise, blockchain can

Prominent Altcoins To Monitor In The Realm Of Digital Currencies

The cryptocurrency industry holds great promise as it continues to gain traction on a global scale, evidenced by the widespread adoption of digital currencies as a legitimate form of payment by numerous businesses. Cryptocurrency serves as a medium of payment and an investment vehicle, akin to contemporary methods of investing such as market shares, mutual funds, precious metals, and real estate. Investors are displaying a growing inclination towards allocating their funds towards cryptocurrencies, thus resulting in a surge in demand for such digital assets, ultimately leading to a substantial appreciation in their prices.

It is imperative to acknowledge that there is no time limit to initiate investments in cryptocurrency. However, it is indeed unfeasible to make investments in Bitcoin due to its astronomically high valuation. Consequently, we are compelled to choose the cryptocurrency that currently exhibits a slightly lower value but has the potential for imminent growth.

There are in excess of 5000 cryptocurrencies worldwide, making it a considerable challenge to identify an appropriate cryptocurrency for investment purposes. Nevertheless, the future trajectory of cryptocurrencies can be gauged by examining their market capitalization, along with other pertinent factors.

What is the concept of cryptocurrency and what are its advantages for utilization?

Cryptocurrencies are a digitized medium of exchange that leverage the underlying structure of the internet. They can be utilized in a multitude of ways that are not feasible with traditional forms of currency. They abstain from depending on conventional financial institutions to authenticate and ensure transactions. Ideally, the validation or verification of cryptocurrency transactions occurs through the user's computer and the overarching currency network. The devices responsible for verifying a transaction usually receive a modest incentive, and the act of receiving compensation in exchange for verifying sales is referred to as "mining." Mining generates fresh currency, whereby the specific methodology employed varies based on the currency in question.

Key Considerations to Assess Prior to Investing or Purchasing Cryptocurrencies

Cryptocurrencies are exchanged through multiple methods and employ diverse algorithms. Before making any decisions to purchase or invest in a cryptocurrency, it is imperative to carefully assess certain fundamental aspects such as the means of verification, widespread acceptance by retailers, and key factors such as its market capitalization and daily trading volume.

Retailer Acceptance

The utilization of cryptocurrencies is rendered impractical in the absence of the ability to make purchases using said digital currencies. Prior to committing any investment in cryptocurrencies, it is imperative for one to ascertain the acceptance of the currency by reputable entities and discern the jurisdiction wherein it holds validity. Certain currencies are designed with objectives that extend beyond the mere facilitation of commercial transactions. While it is true that certain cryptocurrencies are exclusively traded for other varieties of cryptocurrencies, there are several widely recognized cryptocurrencies, such as Bitcoin, that enjoy broad acceptance.

Verification Method

The primary disparities among cryptocurrencies lie in their respective verification mechanisms. Proof of Work (POW) represents one of the earliest and well-established methodologies employed in the verification process of a check. Computational devices are required to allocate substantial time and energy to solve complex mathematical problems in order to acquire the privilege of verifying transactions. Nevertheless, the challenge encountered by a majority of individuals utilizing this approach lies in the substantial energy consumption required for its operation. A Proof-of-Stake system (POS), nevertheless, tries resolving these issues by allowing the user to the large currency share to verify the transactions. The network asserts quicker transaction speeds and utilizes minimal processing power to operate. Nevertheless, due to the prevailing security apprehensions, only a limited number of cryptocurrencies fully depend on Proof-of-Stake systems.

The volume of daily trades and the overall market capitalization

The market capitalization of cryptocurrency can be characterized as the aggregate value encompassing all coins presently in circulation. A significant market capitalization signifies a substantial value assigned to individual coins. It is important to emphasize that the trading volume of a currency on a daily basis holds greater significance than its market capitalization.

Which altcoins show the most promising potential in the realm of cryptocurrencies? Presented herewith is an inventory encompassing the most prominent alternative cryptocurrencies available.

Prior to commencing, I would like to emphasize that the aforementioned listing merely represents a small portion of the comprehensive compilation. For a comprehensive inventory of noteworthy altcoins worthy of attention in 2018 and the foreseeable future, kindly direct your attention to www.4pr100.com/btc.

A selection of noteworthy alternative coins to monitor in 2018 is...

Ethereum

This particular digital currency was developed by Vitalik Buterin, a prodigious mathematician who was 19 years old at the time of its creation. In terms of the hierarchical order of cryptocurrencies, Ethereum holds the second position after Bitcoin. Similar to Bitcoin, Ethereum is distributed on public blockchain networks. Despite the presence of several notable disparities between Ethereum and Bitcoin, the principal disparity lies in their respective capacities and intended functionalities.

Bitcoin has been developed to offer a singular application of blockchain technology, which entails an automated monetary system facilitating online transactions involving Bitcoin. While the blockchain of Bitcoin has the capability to monitor ownership of Bitcoin, the Ethereum blockchain has been specifically designed to prioritize the execution of program codes for decentralized applications. The innovator behind Ethereum adopted a novel methodology that revolutionized various uses, particularly its blockchain infrastructure, and even reshaped the landscape of the internet as we currently perceive it.

The fundamental breakthrough of Ethereum, known as the Ethereum Virtual Machine (EVM), can be characterized as the software responsible for the execution of operations within the Ethereum network. The EVM serves as an intermediary communication layer connecting numerous applications within an Ethereum network. It functions as a protective barrier that safeguards the integrity of individual programs within the blockchain, preventing any form of interference between them, and establishes a secure testing environment for developers to implement new protocols and applications on the Ethereum blockchain.

The creation process for apps is greatly facilitated and remarkably efficient with the usage of EVM. Instead of constructing a completely novel blockchain for each new application, or altering an existing open source blockchain, the Ethereum nodes serve as fundamental hubs where applications can be executed.

In February 2017, the Ethereum organization made an official announcement regarding the development of substantial business solutions through the Enterprise Ethereum Alliance (EEA). Furthermore, numerous corporate entities and companies have commenced their engagement with Ethereum on a daily basis. Among the aforementioned are Samsung, Toyota, Mastercard, Microsoft, JP Morgan, Intel, BP, Scotiabank, National Bank of Canada, and Consensys, to name a few.

How To Buy Nft

In the span of the last three years, there has been a significant upsurge in the valuation of the NFT market, exhibiting substantial growth of nearly ten times its size between 2018 and 2020. The market capitalization of the NFT market experienced a substantial increase, climbing from $40.96 million to $141.56 million in 2019, and subsequently surging to $338.04 million in 2020. Due to its rapidly increasing market capitalization, the NFT market has garnered the interest of prominent investors, venture capitalists, public figures and various influential individuals, as there is a widespread eagerness to partake in the opportunities presented by NFTs.

In addition to the rapidly increasing market capitalization of the non-fungible token (NFT) market, as reported by nonfungible.com, a comprehensive platform tracking NFT data across more than 120 marketplaces, the cumulative sales of NFTs have reached a staggering 5.48 million units, generating a revenue of $542,474,788! If we divide this total revenue by the span of four years, it yields an average of $135,618,697 per year, indicating that the average yearly sales volume stemming from NFT transactions amounts to approximately $135 million.

Notwithstanding this noteworthy statistic, I maintain that there remains a significant potential for growth in the NFT market, particularly when one takes into account the fact that the annual sales volume of $135 million represents only a fraction of the $63.7 billion annual volume generated by conventional art marketplaces. Taking a conservative approach in assessing the annual sales volume that the NFT marketplace is projected to generate in the forthcoming decade, it is anticipated to amount to 10% of the yearly volume seen in the traditional art marketplace. This implies that over the course of the next ten years, the annual sales of NFTs have the potential to reach a substantial sum of $6.3 billion.

The projected annual sales volume of $6.3 billion demonstrates that the present highest record for an NFT sale, the $69 million sale of Beeple's "5000 Everydays," accounts for less than 0.01% of the anticipated yearly sales volume. Consider the implications this holds for future sales of NFTs. It is evident that NFT sales in the million range will become a regular phenomenon within the NFT industry.

Buying NFTs

The purchase and sale transactions take place on specialized NFT market platforms. As a result of the diverse range of NFTs in existence, including art NFTs, trading card NFTs, and virtual land, certain specialized platforms have emerged to primarily facilitate transactions specific to particular types of NFTs. In addition to these primary NFT marketplaces, numerous secondary markets exist wherein you can subsequently resell any NFT acquired from the primary market. Therefore, it is imperative to carefully evaluate the specific nature of the NFT you intend to engage in before selecting an appropriate marketplace that aligns with your NFT transactions.

Allow us to examine a curated assortment of esteemed primary and secondary NFT marketplaces.

OpenSea

This platform was introduced in 2018, rendering it the inaugural decentralized

NFT marketplace within the realms of NFTs. The platform denotes itself as the foremost marketplace for digital goods, offering the opportunity to engage in transactions involving a myriad of distinctive digital items. These distinctive articles may encompass a wide range of items, spanning from virtual assets such as gaming items, domain names, and collectibles, to even encompassing digital manifestations of tangible possessions. In essence, the platform can be described as the NFT equivalent of eBay, as it facilitates the systematic categorization and hosting of a vast array of assets. In addition, it enables users to explore other NFT marketplaces seamlessly within its platform.

Rarible

This platform is headquartered in Moscow and was founded by Alex

Salnikov and Alexei Falin prior to its official launch in early 2020. The platform functions as an exclusive marketplace for art assets, granting users the opportunity to engage in transactions involving a wide range of digital collectibles. In addition to engaging in NFT trading on the platform, users also possess the capability to create and authenticate their own NFTs. It may be helpful to mention that minting refers to the procedure of transforming digital content into a unique and verifiable NFT. Consequently, the platform has garnered a significant number of content creators who convert their music albums, movies, and other works into non-fungible tokens (NFTs) and subsequently offer them for sale on the platform.

Furthermore, aside from minting, creators of content possess the choice of either releasing the complete content of their non-fungible token (NFT) for potential buyers to examine or providing them with a glimpse of the content prior to its full release upon purchase of the NFT. Nevertheless, following numerous encounters with individuals attempting to deceive users through the sale of counterfeit projects, Rarible has implemented a verification procedure aimed at reducing the likelihood of users engaging with fraudulent endeavors.

To date, the platform has garnered the attention of more than 37,000 traders and has effectively generated a trading volume totaling $79.84 million. In addition, notable individuals from the industry, including Linsey Lohan, have shown interest in the platform. Linsey Lohan possesses a presence on the platform and achieved a significant transaction, selling her NFT artwork, "Bitcoin Lightening," for a sum slightly exceeding $50,000, representing one of the most substantial sales on the platform.

Nifty Gateway

Nifty Gateway is a platform established by The Cock Foster Twins and introduced in 2018 prior to its acquisition by Tyler and Cameron Winklevoss, also known as the Winklevoss twins. The platform enables users to acquire digital assets, referred to as Nifties, and conveniently facilitates the acquisition of Nifties for well-known cryptographic games and applications such as Gods Unchained and CryptoKitties.

The platform's seamless NFT purchasing process contributes to its popularity within the NFT ecosystem. Acquiring an NFT through the platform entails the straightforward process of accessing the marketplace via your web browser, selecting a desirable item, inputting your credit card details, and executing the purchase. Subsequently, you may opt to retain the NFT that you have acquired within your Nifty Gateway account, or alternatively, you may determine to transfer it to a wallet of your choice.

Although it is feasible to craft your own unique product for sale on the platform, it is necessary to submit an application for approval prior to doing so. The platform additionally provides creators with the ability to establish royalty rates for their creations. Consequently, whenever one of their creations is subsequently sold, the creator will receive the predetermined rate.

SuperRare

SuperRare is a non-fungible token (NFT) marketplace that was inaugurated in the year 2017. The platform is primarily focused on facilitating the creation of digital art, empowering artists to transform their artwork into non-fungible tokens (NFTs) and subsequently market and sell their creations within the platform's ecosystem.

As a purchaser, your task entails simply choosing any artwork that appeals to you. Subsequently, you have the option to either procure the artwork at the listed price or present an offer through submitting a bid. After the acquisition of the artwork has been accomplished, you may choose to retain it within your collection or proceed with its resale on the secondary market, catering to other art enthusiasts. You have the option to showcase your art collection on the platform, or alternatively, you may choose to exhibit them within a digital gallery, virtual reality gallery, or any other desired location.

As an artist in the pursuit of selling your digital artwork, it is imperative to undergo the process of authentication. This entails affixing your digital signature to the artwork while creating a tokenized certificate that serves as tangible proof of your ownership over the artistic creation. Once your work has been duly verified, you may proceed to establish a predetermined value for your art or alternatively, afford collectors the opportunity to submit bids on your art. Nevertheless, considering that the platform is currently in its early access stage, they are exclusively accepting a limited number of carefully selected artists for onboarding. Despite this, it is still possible for you to fill out a form that may result in an invitation to present your artwork in the near future.

Terra Virtua

Terra Virtua is an engrossing and interactive multi-platform collectible experience that made its debut in 2019. The platform facilitates a cohesive cross-platform ecosystem that spans both augmented reality and virtual reality domains, enabling users to participate in the social, interactive, and immersive experience of sharing, trading, and interacting with digital collectibles.

One has the opportunity to amass exclusive art collectibles crafted by diverse creators and exhibit them in one's private art gallery. Likewise, you can use your digital collectibles as real game items on the platform by utilizing the immersive capabilities provided by the platform. To put it succinctly, Terra Virtua enables users to engage with their digital assets through various mediums such as online platforms, a mobile application, and immersive 3D environments utilizing Augmented Reality and Virtual Reality technologies.

Additionally, the platform possesses its exclusive cryptocurrency known as Kolect, currently trading at a value of $0.7607. This digital asset boasts a circulating supply of 219,201,959 Kolect tokens and maintains a market capitalization of approximately $167.14 million.

NBA Top Shot

NBA Top Shot functions as a Non-Fungible Token marketplace with the endorsement and support of the National Basketball Association (NBA). This platform was introduced in the year 2020 as a marketplace that facilitates the buying and selling of segments featuring NBA gameplay by individuals. In essence, Top Shot transmutes exhilarating highlights into digital collectibles referred to as moments.

Through the process of transforming an action-packed highlight into a non-fungible token (NFT), the purchaser or possessor of said NFT is bestowed with exclusive ownership rights over that specific moment.

Since its inception, the platform has garnered the participation of more than 271,000 traders and has amassed a trade volume of $449.37 million, establishing itself as the premier marketplace in terms of user base and trading activity. Nevertheless, the platform is exclusively devoted to the trading of NBA moments that can be subsequently resold by initial purchasers on any secondary marketplace.

Axie Infinity

Axie Infinity is a decentralized gaming platform that utilizes blockchain technology, displaying resemblances to the CryptoKitties game centered around breeding virtual felines. The game permits players to acquire mythical beings referred to as Axies. These entities possess distinctive non-fungible tokens with specific attributes that grant them substantial value within the confines of the game. Similar to CryptoKitties, Axies have the ability to engage in breeding with other Axies, resulting in the creation of distinct Axies with rare and exclusive attributes. Given that Axies are employed within the game for the purpose of partaking in competitive tournaments, wherein victorious participants are rewarded with cryptocurrency prizes, this endows them with significant value. This is due to the continual pursuit of players in acquiring Axies possessing rare attributes and exhibiting exceptional performance in battle, thereby securing triumphs. In order to emerge victorious in the battle tournament of the game, players must tactfully acquire the NFT game assets to enhance their gaming experience. Consequently, the demand for these NFTs on the platform is exceedingly high.

Foundation

Foundation is a digital collectibles platform that has experienced a substantial increase in usage and presence since its inception in 2020, driven by the active participation of the community. Upon the initial launch of the platform, it extended invitations to a group of 50 artists, with each individual artist subsequently receiving two additional invitations to be shared with subsequent new members of the platform.

AtomicMarket

AtomicMarket is an exclusive platform for Non-Fungible Tokens (NFTs) that seamlessly integrates with the AtomicAssets hub. This NFT marketplace provides its users with the opportunity to create listings for NFTs available for sale or arrange them for auction. Nevertheless, what sets this NFT market apart is the inherent characteristic that, as a seller, you retain ownership of the NFT until it is acquired by a buyer. Let me explain better.

When engaging in the process of listing NFTs for sale on alternate NFT marketplaces, it is incumbent upon the seller to offer the NFT in question for sale on said platforms. Nevertheless, AtomicMarket operates differently whereby the requirement to promptly transfer the NFT to your platform account upon listing for sale is waived. Alternatively, the platform employs a trade offer functionality that allows you to list your NFT for sale. Only upon acceptance and purchase of the asset by a buyer, do you proceed to transfer the NFT to the platform. Consequently, it implies that you have the ability to enlist that specific NFT on alternate platforms or persist in utilizing it within dApps until such time as someone accepts your trade offer on AtomicMarket.

Since its inception in the early months of 2021, the platform has garnered the attention of 35,953 traders who actively participate in its marketplace, thereby generating a commendable total trade volume of $8.64.

The burgeoning demand for NFTs in recent years has precipitated the emergence of numerous NFT marketplaces. There exist certainly numerous auspicious NFT marketplaces in which one can engage in the purchasing and selling of NFTs;

nevertheless, it is imperative to take into account both the trading volume and the quantity of a given marketplace when seeking to procure or vend NFTs. Increased trading volume and a larger user base contribute to the enhanced liquidity of such a marketplace. The following table presents various NFT marketplaces along with their respective trading volumes and the number of users they accommodate. The list can be utilized to ascertain the most liquid marketplace for executing your NFT transactions.

Cryptocurrency And Blockchain

Cryptocurrency

Cryptocurrencies are decentralized forms of currency, devoid of a centralized lending authority such as a nation's central bank. These digital assets employ computer encryption

methodologies to impose constraints on the total quantity of monetary units generated and subsequently authenticate any transaction of the funds subsequent to their inception.

This method of creation is referred to as "mining" owing to its conceptual resemblance to the extraction of gold or other valuable metals. In order to engage in the act of cryptocurrency mining, it is imperative that individuals undertake the task of deciphering and solving progressively intricate algorithms or puzzles. The resolution of these algorithms necessitates a substantial amount of computational capacity. Put differently, there is a monetary investment involved in the process of mining them, thus we are unable to generate value instantaneously and effortlessly. As a consequence, the value of these currencies is safeguarded by mathematical principles rather than being contingent on the authority of a central government or financial institution.

As the adoption of cryptocurrency continues to expand, an accompanying surge in real-world applications becomes evident. Cryptocurrency facilitates transactions encompassing a wide array of commodities, including tangible products, gift certificates, sporting event passes, and even accommodations at hotels. Additionally, selected bars and restaurants have now implemented the acceptance of this form of payment. Several non-governmental organizations (NGOs) have currently adopted the practice of accepting donations in Bitcoin and other forms of digital currency. Additionally, there exist further illegitimate applications, exemplified by clandestine virtual marketplaces engaged in the distribution of unlawful commodities, such as Silk Road and AlphaBay.

These currencies possess a multitude of advantages compared to the currencies widely utilized in contemporary society. This characteristic renders them highly appealing to both enduring investors and immediate speculators. Naturally, similar to any form of investment, cryptocurrencies do possess certain disadvantages - which we shall delve into further in the subsequent chapters of this book.

How it Works

Contrary to commonly held belief, Bitcoin did not serve as the inaugural cryptocurrency. E-gold was launched in the year 1996, a dozen years prior to the publication of the Bitcoin white paper by Satoshi Nakamoto. E-gold was supported by tangible gold reserves and, at its peak, boasted a user base exceeding one million individuals. Due to its anonymous nature and the banking system's lack of adaptation to the digital domain, malevolent individuals found it considerably convenient to employ such technology for illicit activities, ranging from identity theft to money laundering. The centralized nature of E-gold rendered it susceptible to hacking attempts, thereby positioning the system as a significant focal point for cyber attackers. The US government decisively mandated its closure.

Various other types of digital currency have emerged, perhaps with your prior experience in utilizing a few. Individuals have the option to procure Facebook credits, which serve to facilitate access to specific games and programs within the Facebook platform, or to enhance their experience on Farmville. Microsoft Rewards is a formal initiative aimed at providing individuals with digital points as a form of recognition for their utilization of specific services. Indeed, these are cryptocurrencies.

Bitcoin, nevertheless, proved to be a transformative force as it introduced an innovative technological breakthrough known as blockchain. Indeed, the blockchain was purposefully developed for the seamless execution of the Bitcoin protocol. A blockchain is an example of a decentralized software system, which essentially implies that it operates in a manner distinct from systems like e-gold, as it is not governed or controlled by any singular entity. Instead, its functioning extends to thousands of distributed node computers globally. This decentralization yields numerous advantages. One aspect to consider is that hacking can be deemed highly improbable due to the absence of a centralized server to infiltrate. In order for a hacker to exert control, a majority of 51% of the nodes in the blockchain must be compromised. Additionally, an important advantage is that the integrity of the information it holds remains uncompromisable unless, once more, a majority of 51% of the blockchain's nodes is under control. This indicates that the data stored within a blockchain is unchangeable. It cannot be changed. New protocols may be deployed and activated via a process known as a fork, yet the data securely recorded in the blockchain remains irreversibly preserved.

The primary factor contributing to the success of Bitcoin lies in its resolution of the issue of double spending. Double spending refers to the occurrence when a single token is used for two separate transactions, thereby facilitating deceptive and illegitimate transactions. The verification mechanism devised by Nakamoto encompasses a concept known as proof of work, which effectively mitigates the risk of double spending.

While new dollars are generated through government intervention such as adjusting interest rates or increasing the money supply (which can result in inflation), the creation of new cryptocurrency tokens is solely dependent on their active utilization by individuals. Certain cryptocurrencies, such as XRP, are designed in a manner that prohibits the creation of any additional units, ensuring that the only coins in circulation are those that were initially generated upon the program's inception. However, the majority of individuals utilize the mining process as a means of generating fresh tokens.

Mining serves as the procedural means by which cryptocurrency transactions undergo verification, thereby ensuring a sustained alignment between supply and demand dynamics. Hence, the intrinsic worth of the aforementioned currency surpasses that of the dollar, which is subject to government influence in terms of its valuation. Evidently, cryptocurrency possesses the characteristics of currency, arguably embodying a more genuine and authentic manifestation of monetary value than traditional fiat currencies such as dollars.

Blockchain

The blockchain denotes an ever-expanding registry of transactions. The blocks present on the blockchain are connected to the transactions that are executed on cryptocurrency platforms like Ethereum or Bitcoin. Each block comprises a hash pointer establishing its linkage to the preceding block. Each transaction will be assigned a time stamp, enabling users to discern the exact moment at which the transaction was accepted into the chain.

The early 1990s witnessed the pioneering development of secure blockchains by Stuart Haber and W. Scott Stornetta. Both students collaborated on conducting research on Merkle trees in order to explore the possibility of developing a more streamlined method for aggregating data from a singular block.

The initial inception of blockchain technology was conceptualized by an individual affiliated with the Satoshi Nakamoto group in 2008, during their endeavors towards developing the fundamental elements of Bitcoin's public ledger. The blockchain is interconnected with a decentralized network, which upon application of a time stamp to a transaction, will be dispersed across a server.

The management of the blockchain database is conducted autonomously. Therefore, when employing the blockchain technology for cryptocurrencies such as Bitcoin, it can be assured that instances of double spending will not transpire unless expressly permitted by you or an authorized administrator.

The term blockchain was initially introduced in a research paper published in 2008 by an individual affiliated with the Nakamoto group. Subsequently, the concept was widely adopted to designate a platform for cryptocurrencies. In the year 2014, the size of Bitcoin's blockchain file amounted to 20 GB. Currently, the record stands at more than 100 gigabytes.

The term "Blockchain 2.0" was coined to refer to the implementation of novel applications on the distributed database of Blockchain. It was characterized as a programming language through which users could author highly refined smart contracts. After drafting the smart contract, an invoice shall be generated to facilitate payment upon fulfillment of the essential terms of the agreement. The blockchain technologies of version 2.0 have transcended mere transactions, evolving to function as intermediaries for both finance and data.

The original intention behind the creation of blockchain technology was to offer individuals the option to safeguard their privacy and commercially benefit from their information, all the while guaranteeing appropriate compensation to the creators for their intellectual contributions.

The second iteration of blockchain technology facilitated the storage of a user's digital identity and persona, while simultaneously offering a viable solution to address the issue of social inequality. In the year 2016, a novel protocol was introduced, wherein an off-chain oracle was endowed with the capability to acquire data and observations that lie beyond the confines of the network, thus enabling it to forecast the prevailing market conditions. This facilitated seamless interaction between the blockchain and the market in a synchronized manner.

The Russian Federation made an official declaration regarding their intention to deploy Blockchain's platform for the purpose of electronic voting. The music industry has adopted blockchain technology for the purpose of issuing royalties and maintaining copyright records.

Blocks on the blockchain that are not chosen for inclusion in the chain are referred to as orphan blocks. Colleagues are poised to provide backing to the various iterations of the blocks over time. The database will retain solely the version with the highest score, as all other versions will be overwritten prior to their distribution to peers for refinement. There can be no assurance that the entry of the block will be retained; nevertheless, this will prevent the blocks from overwriting one another and resulting in the placement of duplicate data on the blockchain.

How Blockchain works

When data is stored within a network, the blockchain engenders the elimination of vulnerabilities associated with centralized information storage. Given that the blockchain operates in a decentralized manner, it will be necessary to utilize spontaneous messages within the distributed network.

The network of blockchain is expected to be devoid of susceptible areas that cyber attackers can capitalize on within a centralized system. The security of blockchain will encompass techniques such as the utilization of public key cryptography. Public keys consist of an alphanumeric string that serves to uniquely identify every user. The public key will be transmitted to an individual seeking to send you digital currency.

The value tokens transmitted through a blockchain network serve to document any information associated with that particular address. Private keys will be associated with a password, ensuring exclusive access to users' assets and preventing unauthorized entry. It is imperative that you maintain exclusive possession of your private key, as its compromise would grant unauthorized individuals with a major component necessary for unauthorized access to your digital currency and other assets.

An alternative perspective on private and public keys can be likened to one's telephone number and the corresponding passcode used to unlock the device. Your phone number functions as the public key, as it is known to certain individuals; meanwhile, the passcode to your phone is kept confidential to prevent unauthorized access.

Systems that are centralized in nature are subject to control by a central governing body, leading to the possibility of data manipulation. However, in the event of decentralization, all members of the network will have accessibility to the data, ensuring transparency and eliminating the possibility of concealing information from users.

Each and every node within the blockchain system will possess a replicated version of the blockchain. The integrity of the data will be upheld through the utilization of both the database and a computational trust mechanism. A centralized copy will not be present, hence no user will be regarded as more trustworthy than another. Transactions will be disseminated across the network, rendering them visible to all participants. Messages are sent out on a best effort basis, wherein mining nodes make efforts to validate transactions and create blocks before broadcasting them to other nodes. This enables the verification of the operation and subsequent construction of a block from another node. Blockchain systems utilize timestamp schemes in order to serialize modifications made within the system. Two additional mechanisms employed within the blockchain ecosystem include proof of stake and evidence of burn.

The expansion of the blockchain will lead to a potential centralization of nodes due to the increasing computational resources necessary for managing larger data files. Consequently, this development is anticipated to incur elevated costs.

CHAPTER 2

2.1 The Significance of Acquiring Knowledge about Cryptocurrency and Essential Information to Familiarize Yourself With

I am confident that you are already aware of the answer to this question by this point. I will reiterate once more, it is a lucrative opportunity. You have the potential to amass a great deal of wealth. Let us examine the factors that contributed to the rapid and substantial rise in the value of this currency within a brief timeframe.

Despite being recognized by several cryptographers as early as 2009, the adoption of cryptocurrencies by the general population required an accessible method to be established. That is where the illicit digital marketplace known as Silk Road comes into play. Throughout the duration spanning from 2011 to 2013, during a period of two and a half years. The exclusive form of payment accepted by Silk Road was limited to Bitcoin. This was due to the fact that Bitcoin transactions offered the advantages of anonymity, security, irreversibility, and global accessibility, enabling trading capabilities across any location with an Internet connection.

According to the FBI, Silk Road had close to one million registered users at the time of its closure in October 2013. Based on this information, it can be inferred that a minimum of one million individuals were likely utilizing Bitcoin exclusively on that particular website. Despite the closure of Silk Road, Bitcoin persevered. At that juncture, a sufficient number of individuals recognized the advantages associated with the utilization of cryptocurrency, not solely for illicit purposes, but as a novel investment opportunity and a form of digital currency with seemingly boundless prospects.

Over the course of the previous year, there has been a notable surge in the level of interest surrounding Bitcoin, and it is presently being utilized by a subset of significantly more reputable individuals. The narrative surrounding Bitcoin has been featured prominently on the covers of a multitude of esteemed publications, such as Time, Newsweek, Forbes, and Bloomberg Businessweek. Over the course of the past three weeks, The New York Times has produced significantly more than twelve articles on the subject of Bitcoin. Google unveiled its "Year in Search" for 2017 on December 13th, disclosing that the second most popular "what is" query in the United States was "What is Bitcoin?" It trailed behind the top searched question, "What is DACA?"

As the public fervor surrounding Bitcoin intensifies to unprecedented levels, presented herein is a comprehensive overview encompassing the historical trajectory, current state, and inherently unpredictable trajectory of Bitcoin and the broader world of cryptocurrency.

2.2 What are the contrasting aspects between cryptocurrency and physical currency such as cash?

The currency is entirely digitized and incorporates several security measures to deter unauthorized access and theft. However, a primary appeal of this novel currency is its independence from reliance on third-party banking or financial institutions. Bitcoin operates in a decentralized manner, where its security is not reliant on human intervention or trust, but rather on mathematical principles, most notably robust cryptography, which ensures secure communication. This is why it is referred to as a cryptocurrency.

Cryptocurrencies employ an intricate cryptographic methodology for the purpose of monitoring and facilitating the exchange of digital currency. This methodology relies on a digital ledger known as a "block chain." In essence, a block chain, or "digital ledger," is a means by which multiple individuals can collectively maintain a comprehensive register of all transactions. It would bear resemblance to a scenario wherein every individual possessed a digitally interconnected notebook.

Whenever an individual inscribes an entry, documenting the acquisition or disposal of an object, the words manifest themselves within your personal ledger as well as the ledgers possessed by others. Additionally, this notebook incorporates security measures that dissuade individuals from providing inaccurate information regarding their acquisitions or making purchases exceeding their financial means.

Please take into account the following rationales

Resistant to fraudulent activities: Upon the creation of a cryptocurrency, all validated transactions are securely recorded in a publicly accessible ledger. The identities of coin owners are subjected to encryption measures to guarantee the integrity of record preservation. As a result of the decentralized nature of the currency, ownership is attributed to you. Both the government and the bank lack any authority over it.

Identity Theft: The ledger guarantees the ability to accurately calculate the balance for all transactions involving "digital wallets". All transactions undergo verification to ensure that the coins being utilized are in possession of the present spender. This public ledger is alternatively known as a "transaction block chain". Block chain technology guarantees secure digital transactions by implementing encryption and "smart contracts," rendering the entity highly impervious to hacking attempts and completely devoid of fraudulent activity. With such robust security measures in place, the potential of blockchain technology to revolutionize various aspects of our daily lives is substantial.

Immediate Finalization: The value of cryptocurrency stems from the utilization of blockchain technology. The high demand for cryptocurrency can be attributed to its user-friendly nature. With the possession of a smart device and access to the internet, individuals can promptly assume the role of their own financial institution, facilitating transactions and conducting monetary transfers.

Readily available: A vast population of more than two billion individuals worldwide possesses Internet connectivity, yet lacks the privilege to engage in conventional financial platforms. These individuals possess a comprehensive understanding and knowledge of the cryptocurrency market.

2.3 What is blockchain?

This article aims to provide a comprehensive analysis of the impact of blockchain technology on the market. Given that it is the foundational mechanism underlying the functionality of cryptocurrency.

A blockchain, initially referred to as a block chain, is an ever-expanding catalogue of records, known as blocks, that interconnect and ensure security through the application of cryptography. Typically, within every block there is the inclusion of a cryptographic hash of the preceding block, a timestamp, and transaction data. By virtue of its inherent design, a blockchain possesses an inherent resistance to any form of data modification. It is an openly accessible and decentralized ledger capable of efficiently documenting transactions between two parties, ensuring their verifiability and permanence. A blockchain is commonly administered by a decentralized network of peers that collectively follow a prescribed communication protocol and validate the addition of new blocks, as a means to facilitate its operation as a distributed ledger. After being recorded, the data within a specific block cannot be retroactively modified unless all subsequent blocks are altered, necessitating the collusion of the majority of the network.

Blockchains possess inherent security measures and exemplify a distributed computing system that exhibits substantial Byzantine fault tolerance. With the utilization of a blockchain, a state of decentralized consensus has thus been attained. Blockchains exhibit potential for effectively recording various activities, such as events, medical records, and other management endeavors like identity management, transaction processing, documenting provenance, food traceability, or voting.

The blockchain is an undeniably brilliant innovation, conceived by an individual or collective entity under the pseudonym, Satoshi Nakamoto. However, it has since undergone significant transformation, prompting each individual to inquire: What precisely is block chain?

Through the facilitation of digital information distribution while preventing unauthorized duplication, blockchain technology has established the fundamental structure of a novel form of internet. The technology was initially developed for utilization in the digital currency known as Bitcoin. However, it has since garnered the attention of the tech community, which is currently exploring alternative applications and potential uses for this innovative technology.

Bitcoin is commonly referred to as "the digital equivalent of gold," and this comparison holds substantial merit. As of now, the cumulative value of the currency amounts to approximately $9 billion USD. Furthermore, blockchains have the capability to generate various forms of digital assets. Similar to the internet or an automobile, one does not necessarily require an in-depth understanding of the mechanics underlying the blockchain in order to effectively utilize it. Nevertheless, possessing a fundamental understanding of this emerging

technology elucidates the reason behind its categorization as revolutionary.

Digital Currencies And Decentralized Digital Assets

Digital currencies are electronic forms of decentralized mediums of exchange that function as a ledger system. On the other hand, conventional forms of currency such as physical banknotes and coins are manually exchanged and are governed by governmental issuance and backing. Despite the increasing prominence of digital currencies, the inception of digital monetary systems can be traced back to the early 1990s. Concurrently, the Internet remained a relatively nascent phenomenon that the general populace was endeavoring to grasp.

Various companies and programmers made endeavors to establish digital currency during the period of the 1990s and early 2000s, encompassing notable efforts such as those undertaken by DigiCash and Flooz. Nevertheless, as a result of inadequate technological infrastructure, inadequate security measures, financial limitations, and a myriad of other obstacles, a significant number of these initial currencies encountered difficulties in gaining widespread recognition and adoption. Nevertheless, certain elements of their technologies and inventive concepts persist in contemporary digital currencies.

Figure 1. Digital Currency Timeline

Bitcoin heralded the dawn of the cryptocurrency era. The concept was first deliberated upon in a scholarly publication entitled "Bitcoin: A Peer-to-Peer Electronic Cash System", which was published online under the name of Satoshi Nakamoto, potentially his genuine identity or an alias. The deployment of the Bitcoin network protocol occurred approximately two months subsequent to that, specifically on the third of January in the year 2009. This technological milestone gave rise to the emergence of a decentralized public ledger. It facilitates international money transfers without necessitating validation from a third-party entity. In the contemporary era, there exist numerous alternative cryptocurrencies characterized by diverse functionalities and specifications. Certain ones among these are replicas and variations of Bitcoin, whereas others derive from either forks or novel cryptocurrencies that originated from pre-existing ones.

Subsequently, a multitude of individuals from various nations have encountered or come across cryptocurrencies. Since the emergence of Bitcoin, there has been a proliferation of numerous cryptocurrencies in the subsequent years. These cryptocurrencies were labeled as "alternative" subsequent to the emergence of Bitcoin, as they were designed, implemented, and evolved to serve as supplementary or potential substitutes for Bitcoin. In the context of Bitcoin, it could be contended that there exists a matter of selecting a particular brand. These findings have been achieved through oral communication, unintended circumstances, individual research, or through information disseminated by the media. Nevertheless, a considerable number of individuals have experienced significant life changes as a consequence thereof. This phenomenon has triggered a substantial surge in inquiries from the public on a wide range of subjects encompassing economics, politics, philosophy, mathematics, and various other academic disciplines.

Since the emergence of Bitcoin and Ethereum, an increasing number of individuals have either already allocated or are planning to allocate their investments towards cryptocurrencies. They are actively seeking a cryptocurrency specifically tailored to their needs and preferences. A comprehensible cryptocurrency that resonates with their sensibilities. They are seeking more than mere monetary value; rather, they aspire to foster a transformative societal force.

The fundamental definition of cryptocurrency is akin to a conventional currency within the market, albeit purely digital in nature. It is a digital currency that employs cryptographic mechanisms for the purpose of ensuring security. This particular currency possesses intricate measures that render it highly resistant to counterfeiting. The majority of cryptocurrencies exhibit a decentralized nature as they operate on blockchain technology, which is essentially a distributed ledger created by an intricate network of computer systems. The primary distinguishing characteristic of cryptocurrencies lies in their inherent organic nature, as they are not issued by any central authority. It confers upon it a theoretical exemption from government rules and regulations.

In addition, these systems facilitate online transactions that ensure a higher level of payment security. It is expressed in units of a virtual token, symbolizing transaction records that define its presence within the system. The term "crypto" pertains to its utilization of encryption algorithms and cryptographic techniques like elliptical curves, public-private key pairs, and hashes.

The initial instance of cryptocurrency gaining popularity arose with the introduction of Bitcoin in 2009, spearheaded by a team under the pseudonym of Satoshi Nakamoto. Amidst the proliferation of cryptocurrencies in the marketplace, the digital ecosystem witnessed the accumulation of 18 million Bitcoins, which currently possess a collective market value of approximately 115 billion dollars, notwithstanding periodic fluctuations in their market price. The triumph of Bitcoin subsequently gave rise to multiple cryptocurrencies aimed at rivaling its position. These cryptocurrencies were commonly referred to as altcoins, exemplified by Litecoin, Peercoin, Ethereum, and Namecoin. At present, the realm of cryptocurrencies encompasses a myriad of options, with an amassed market worth surpassing 200 billion dollars.

How To Market Your Drop-Shipping Store

So far, this book has thoroughly covered all aspects related to drop-shipping, including various types of drop-shipping enterprises, the process of establishing one's own drop-shipping business, and the methods for identifying the most lucrative niche and products. It is imperative to recognize that every element plays a crucial role in the success of your business. However, if you are unable to attract individuals to visit your webpage or generate substantial traffic, all the knowledge provided in this book will be ineffective in facilitating sales. It is essential to note that without an audience or potential customers witnessing your product or the offering you have, the likelihood of any sales or purchases is greatly diminished. It will simply remain idle and unproductive. In this chapter, we will discuss the methods by which you can effectively generate footfall or online traffic to your store or webpage, thus facilitating sales.

Acquiring the knowledge to generate traffic can prove to be a formidable undertaking. There are no definitive correct or incorrect answers within this approach. Certain individuals may find great success by utilizing platforms such as Facebook and Instagram, solely relying on these websites to generate traffic. Conversely, others may achieve impressive sales through the implementation of complimentary traffic techniques that come at no cost. Therefore, it can be regarded as a process of experimentation rather than achieving success on the initial attempt.

Upon embarking on my drop-shipping venture, I diligently explored an array of marketing strategies, encompassing Facebook ads in addition to leveraging organic traffic techniques such as blog creation and email campaigns. However, each of my drop-shipping enterprises operates distinctively, with some yielding substantial Facebook traffic, others excelling in generating blog traffic or email-based conversions. Therefore, the success of each business is contingent upon this contextual variance. In order to ascertain the efficacy and ineffectiveness, it is imperative that you engage in practical experimentation and personally observe the outcomes. It is impossible to determine with certainty whether a particular advertisement will yield millions of dollars or not.

We will discuss the three most notable methods for increasing traffic to your product page or website - specifically, through the utilization of Facebook ads, Instagram shout outs, and harnessing free traffic via blogs, emails, and similar avenues. Prior to forming a judgment, please endeavor to test each option before dismissing any of them. As previously mentioned, certain options may prove to be exceptionally effective for your needs in comparison to the alternative choices, which warrants thorough exploration and experimentation. Having considered all of the aforementioned, we shall commence our efforts by addressing the most challenging issue at hand, namely Facebook.

Facebook

Facebook boasts an extensive user base, surpassing a staggering figure of 2 billion active users. There exists a considerable number of individuals on Facebook who exhibit a strong inclination towards the acquisition of your merchandise. The Facebook advertisement has been utilized by a substantial number of drop-shippers to effectively direct traffic, and it is deemed as one of the most cost-efficient methods for driving traffic to your product page or store. Now, there are several procedures that need to be followed in order to effectively promote your product via Facebook, which will be thoroughly covered in this chapter.

To commence, upon establishing your Facebook ads account, it is imperative to ensure the incorporation of your website pixel. This holds greater significance for individuals who employ the online drop-shipping method. Here is the thing. Failure to include your store pixel in your Facebook ads account will result in the inability to gather data related to your website and offerings. The pixel will collect valuable insights regarding the demographic profile of visitors to your product page, as well as those who convert to actual purchases. This information will be instrumental in optimizing future ad campaigns, enabling you to precisely target your desired audience for your product page or website. Now that you have successfully set up your Facebook ads account and integrated your pixel with it, we may proceed with the promotion of your products. Outlined below are the matters that require attention prior to commencing our advertising efforts on Facebook.

- Discovering goods similar to yours

Identifying advertising campaigns on Facebook undertaken by large corporations
- Focusing on a specific demographic and geographic region - Tailoring to a particular age range and nation - Directing efforts towards a specific population segment and country - Concentrating on a particular age bracket and country of interest

Exceptional product imagery
- Absolutely astonishing headline - A truly remarkable title - An awe-inspiring caption - A headline of unparalleled excellence - A breathtaking and remarkable caption

- Experimenting with different variations - Conducting A/B tests - Carrying out controlled experiments - Implementing iterative testing approaches

I am aware that there are numerous factors that may be cause for concern. However, it may come as a surprise that these considerations merely represent the fundamental aspects to be addressed, given the existence of numerous alternative advertising strategies. For the time being, address your attention to the fundamental principles.

Thus, let us commence with the initial stage. It is imperative to conduct a thorough search on Google for products similar to yours, as this will often reveal the leading sellers within your specific market. Upon commencing your Facebook advertising campaign, you will be prompted to identify relevant ad pages or entities within your niche. The task at hand is relatively straightforward, albeit significant. Our initial step involves accessing the internet to conduct a thorough search for our desired product. As an illustration, in the case of selling a car, I would conduct a search for "automobiles available for purchase," subsequently requesting you to access each of the platforms offering your merchandise. Therefore, in this imaginary situation, I would be navigating through the websites of Honda, Toyota, and other relevant brands. Following that, I kindly request that you compile a list of all the websites that are relevant to your specific industry or product, which you intend to sell.

Once you have recorded all the prominent websites, kindly proceed to access Facebook. Subsequently, I request you to search for the respective Facebook pages of the aforementioned sites. After completing that task, verify if the number of Facebook likes exceeds

500,000. If it does, you have discovered a successful contender. You observe, Facebook's utilization of this information within your campaign entails the strategic promotion of your product to a targeted demographic on that particular page. Returning to the hypothetical situation at hand... By including Honda in the criteria of my targeted Facebook advertisement for the sale of a car, I can effectively narrow down the audience to individuals with a specific interest in Honda. Therefore, locate a product and corresponding Facebook page boasting a follower count exceeding 500,000, subsequently proceeding to promote the said product to the audience engaged with said page.

Having obtained the relevant keywords and identified the specific target audience for your product, the next step entails crafting a visually appealing advertisement. Given that it is probable that a majority of individuals present have not yet generated a Facebook advertisement, I infer that in order to ascertain the efficacy of your promotional materials in yielding sales, it is imperative that your advertisements possess an aesthetically pleasing appearance. Currently, there exist numerous strategies and methodologies shared by purported experts in the field of drop-shipping. However, it is possible that some of you are familiar with the adage "if it ain't broke, don't fix it." This proverb implies that if prominent companies are effectively promoting their products, there is no necessity to devise one's own distinctive approach. Engaging in trial and error could potentially result in financial harm.

If one meticulously conducted research and diligently sought out prominent websites or corporations within their niche, it is highly probable that they would have encountered the manifestation of these entities' Facebook advertisements. Upon your next encounter, I would appreciate it if you could carefully scrutinize their advertising materials to assess the nature of videos or images they are employing. This will assist you in constructing your own advertisement, therefore it is imperative that you thoroughly examine the advertisements and replicate the methodologies employed. Please believe me when I say that it will be significantly more effective than if you were to design a custom one yourself.

Allow us to address the topic of targeting age demographics and geographical regions for your advertising campaigns. If one possesses an understanding of the benefits that their product offers to consumers, they would possess the knowledge of the specific demographic that would display interest in acquiring their products. Prior to commencing your inaugural Facebook campaign, it will necessitate that you designate an age bracket for your advertisement. Therefore, if one intends to engage in the sale of automobiles, it would be advisable to establish an age demographic of approximately 25 to 65, as this age range encompasses the majority of prospective buyers. Given that the majority of individuals aged 18 will not be making independent purchases of such items, nor will individuals above the age of 65. Our objective is to accurately identify and reach out to the target audience who exhibit the highest propensity for purchasing your product. Therefore, conducting thorough research and employing educated estimations is necessary. By specifying the age requirement precisely, you can effectively optimize cost savings while increasing sales.

If one must choose a county or region to target advertisements, I would suggest solely focusing on the United States of America if there are constraints on the budget. The majority of your prospective buyers will originate from the United States, hence there is no necessity to concern yourself with promoting it to other demographics. If you happen to possess surplus funds, considering extending your outreach towards Canada can potentially yield increased viewership and bolster sales figures.

Upon completion of your extensive research, the next step in the process involves the development of your advertising image and accompanying caption. Many individuals fail to appreciate the significance of selecting an appropriate image and caption for one's social media post. This has the potential to either elevate the quality of your post or undermine it significantly. Therefore, the selection of the appropriate photograph and accompanying caption is crucial for the effectiveness of your advertisement. Now, how does one select the appropriate image for their advertisement? If you diligently conducted thorough research on the websites of prominent companies, you would be able to discern the precise style of photographs or captions to employ, and thus emulate their advertising strategies.

Now that you have made your selections of the photographs and accompanying captions, it is time to proceed with incorporating an image into your campaign. It is imperative to bear in mind that the photo must meet the criteria of being in high-definition. Failure to possess high-definition capabilities would render it inconspicuous among others and exude an unprofessional appearance. Additionally, ensure that the image is compatible with the advertising format of smartphones. To preview the display on a smartphone, please click on the option labeled "smartphone advertisement." It will provide a visual representation.

Next, let us delve into the matter of the caption. To ensure maximum engagement with the caption, it is imperative to make it visually appealing, prompting individuals to click on it. In order to facilitate the delivery of the product, it is essential to provide your clients with additional incentives, such as offering a 50% discount for immediate purchase or highlighting limited availability with only 50 units remaining. Similar to large corporations, it is imperative that you instill a sense of urgency by introducing an enticing incentive.

Ultimately, once all preparations have been completed and the project is fully eligible for implementation, you will proceed to employ a technique known as split testing. Your task entails the creation of two analogous advertising campaigns, incorporating subtle variations. As an illustration, one advertisement may be targeted towards individuals within the age range of 18-50 while the other advertisement may be tailored to those aged between 25-65. After a sufficient period of running the advertisement, it will elucidate the superior performing option in contrast to the alternative, thereby facilitating the optimization of your advertising campaigns in subsequent endeavors. Participation in this activity is discretionary; however, it is strongly advised.

We have covered everything pertaining to Facebook advertising. Let us proceed to discuss the topic of advertising with Instagram influencers.

Instagram

Instagram serves as an exceptional platform for product promotion, showcasing a vast user base that demonstrates remarkably higher levels of engagement in comparison to Facebook. Therefore, reconsider the notion of disregarding the prospect of advertising on Instagram, as doing so would result in missed opportunities. Please be advised that Facebook advertising content appears on Instagram as well, albeit with less effectiveness than anticipated. When engaging in advertising campaigns on Instagram, we employ a strategy known as 'Instagram influencer marketing.' This approach is relatively straightforward. Initially, you will encounter an Instagram page that is pertinent to your subject matter. Additionally, you may solicit their assistance in endorsing your product on their Instagram page, ultimately resulting in an increase in sales. I have experimented with a variety of strategies, however, this particular approach consistently yields successful outcomes! If you seek expeditious sales growth on your Instagram platform, I highly recommend implementing this methodology. Now, let us delve into the considerations that demand your attention prior to commencing advertising efforts on Instagram.

- Locate the appropriate influencer - Discover the ideal influencer - Identify the suitable influencer - Ascertain the fitting influencer - Determine the suitable influencer
- Ensure they do not possess any automated software or BOTs.
- Involvement - Participation - Active participation - Commitment - Dedication - Enthusiasm - Investment - Contribution - Integration - Immersion

So, we present to you the opportunity to generate sales and attain a substantial financial return from those sales. It is imperative to ensure that the influencer you choose possesses an audience that aligns with the desired demographic. It follows that one should not anticipate

132

generating sales from a dog bracelet if the webpage is primarily focused on expressing disdain towards dogs. Do you grasp the essence of my argument? Ensure that the product you are attempting to market is pertinent to the targeted audience on the specific webpage. For instance, if I were interested in selling a fishing rod, I would conduct research to identify online platforms focused on fishing enthusiasts, where I could effectively promote my product.

Prior to embarking on the search for an influencer page, it is imperative to ascertain that the page boasts a minimum of 300k followers. If this is not the case, you will not achieve the desired level of engagement.

The subsequent matter to address would involve ensuring that the influencer with whom you are contemplating collaborating exhibits a considerably elevated level of engagement. If individuals fail to engage with his/her page, it is likely that your advertisements will go unnoticed by the same audience. There exist various techniques at one's disposal to ascertain this, however, if an individual fails to garner a minimum of 5-10% of likes from their followers, specifically if they have 100,000 followers but receive less than 5,000-10,000 likes, it is highly likely that their followers are lacking engagement.

This would also serve to ascertain whether the followers are automated accounts or genuine ones, indicating whether they have been acquired through purchases or earned organically.

Now, let us discuss the strategies to obtain endorsements from these Instagram accounts. Kindly initiate direct communication with them, expressing your request for a shout out. Subsequently, when an agreement has been reached, kindly request a "story shout out" from them, as this advertising method proves to be highly effective. Specify a duration of 12 hours for the story shout out, ensuring that all of their followers will be exposed to your advertisement within this time frame, thereby obviating the need to prolong the advertising period unnecessarily.

Having made that statement, we shall now proceed to examine the third approach.

Locating Your Individual Bitcoin Solution

This section is anticipated to be the most intricate in terms of Bitcoin. This can be attributed to the absence of a distinct elucidation regarding the mechanisms and potential benefits of Bitcoin mining for its user base. There exist numerous methodologies for Bitcoin mining, and individuals have discovered alternative approaches that yield superior results compared to those utilized by others. While engaging in Bitcoin mining holds significant potential for profitability, it is imperative to undertake this venture solely if one possesses the requisite expertise in technology and mathematics, as well as a substantial amount of time to devote to the pursuit.

Through the process of Bitcoin mining, one can potentially amass considerable wealth, albeit requiring substantial dedication in terms of time investment.

As an illustration, certain individuals may allocate an entire week exclusively to attaining a solitary Bitcoin.

Community Aspect

Bitcoin is enveloped by a robust community. This can be attributed to the limited familiarity and ownership of Bitcoin among a relatively small portion of the global population. Due to the compact nature of the community, a collective effort is made by all members to accomplish tasks.

In order for Bitcoin to function effectively, it is imperative to have the resolution of specific mathematical problems. All of these are generated via algorithms, resulting in encrypted financial gains. In the event that miners are capable of accomplishing this task, they will be able to decipher the code associated with Bitcoin.

The community ensured that mining for it would be accessible to all. This facilitates the resolution of the codes while simultaneously providing individuals with the incentive necessary to independently discover their own Bitcoin. Even individuals with limited financial resources have the capacity to commence their investment ventures in Bitcoin; however, they must possess the requisite knowledge and understanding.

The Basics

To engage in Bitcoin mining, individuals must access the database and conduct numerous queries to identify and address the computational challenges at hand. These matters are intricate and may entail the scrutiny and resolution of numerous cases in order to identify a Bitcoin code with potential. It is an undertaking that, if performed manually, would necessitate an astounding number of hours just to locate a single instance. In its early stages, Bitcoin exhibited a relative simplicity.

Upon acquiring knowledge about mining, individuals resolved to initiate the development of machinery facilitating their pursuit of mining

Bitcoin. This predominantly entailed computer-related tasks, which frequently encompassed the construction of bespoke systems to facilitate the engineering of optimal mining machinery. It is a practice that continues to be undertaken by individuals, with the majority of miners possessing meticulously devised systems exclusively dedicated to the pursuit of locating Bitcoin. They possess fully equipped computer systems and network infrastructures specifically designed for the purpose of Bitcoin mining.

The machinery is frequently constructed starting from the ground up, utilizing the Raspberry Pi systems that enable individuals to develop their own customized software.

As a Miner

A significant proportion of individuals engaged in Bitcoin mining initially pursued it as a recreational pursuit. Subsequent to their initial Bitcoin discovery, they were able to leverage the resultant funds to facilitate further development. It served as a catalyst for their determination towards the discovery of Bitcoin. Certain individuals possess highly sophisticated systems that are remarkably adept at identifying and acquiring Bitcoin, enabling them to engage in the occupation of full-time Bitcoin mining as their primary means of income. Subsequently, individuals have the capacity to allocate their earnings into investments, owing to the incessant appreciation of Bitcoin's value.

A significant proportion of miners presently experiencing consistent high yields of Bitcoin are those who initially embarked on the mining activity. Approximately half of the individuals presently engaged in Bitcoin mining were among the initial cohort of Bitcoin miners. They have acquired the skillset necessary to identify optimal mathematical challenges, develop effective algorithms, and maximize the financial gains derived from the Bitcoin they have discovered.

Help from Bitcoin

Although Bitcoin cannot directly assist miners in their search, it does have the potential to provide individuals with certain benefits. The greater their possession of Bitcoin, the more they stand to gain from the various computer systems they can financially support for their diverse pursuits.

While possessing significant wealth in Bitcoin does not necessarily facilitate the acquisition of additional Bitcoin, it does afford individuals the opportunity to develop more intricate and sophisticated machinery. Once they acquire the most advanced machinery, they will consequently maximize their Bitcoin yield through the utilization of said machinery for mining purposes.

The involvement of the individuals responsible for the inception of Bitcoin in the current state of the cryptocurrency is minimal. Even in the event of their significant involvement, their knowledge of the mathematical problems would not encompass all the answers. This is because the creators of Bitcoin devised a system that ensures equitable opportunities for all individuals to acquire the currency. Provided that an individual possesses the requisite expertise to construct the apparatus and possesses the necessary proficiency to address the challenges typically associated with most Bitcoin mining ventures, they can allocate funds into Bitcoin and thereby generate profits.

Bitcoin is undeniably a platform that provides equal opportunities for all individuals.

You Need Hardware

It is highly improbable to engage in Bitcoin mining without the requisite hardware due to the significant number of individuals presently involved in such mining activities. In earlier times, individuals possessed the ability to engage in manual extraction, resolve the associated challenges, and even locate it in diverse regions. That assertion is no longer accurate, and it poses a significant disadvantage for individuals lacking the necessary hardware to procure it. It is not possible to generate a reliable source of income through the practice of Bitcoin mining.

Fortunately, in the event that you possess one Bitcoin, or have indeed dedicated an excessive amount of time in pursuit of a solitary Bitcoin, you possess the funds requisite for the establishment of your own apparatus. Typically, procuring a Raspberry Pi system and establishing its functionality is anticipated to incur expenses in the vicinity of a few hundred dollars, a significantly smaller amount compared to the prevailing value of Bitcoin in 2017.

Acquiring a single unit of Bitcoin offers the potential to establish a personal mining operation, thereby yielding a considerable quantity of Bitcoin that can be monetized.

Starting Out

The majority of individuals embarking on their journey will possess a fundamental understanding of computer-based skills. They will possess the knowledge and skills to effectively configure hardware and possess a working understanding of the essential requirements for proficiently carrying out Bitcoin mining operations across various dimensions.

If one intends to engage in Bitcoin mining, it would be advantageous to explore various alternatives. There exist numerous platforms enabling individuals to simulate the mining process, thereby providing valuable insights into the practical utilization of one's existing or prospective Bitcoin holdings.

It is imperative to ensure that you are adequately prepared before commencing the process of Bitcoin mining. Not only will you be required to invest your money, but you will also need to commit a substantial amount of time to this endeavor. It is imperative to allocate a significant amount of time towards diligently searching for Bitcoin and engaging in the construction of machines intended to facilitate its discovery. Regardless of your location or Bitcoin-related activities, it is impermissible to engage in mining without proper considerations.

Acquire a comprehensive understanding of Bitcoin mining and subsequently engage in the practice to circumvent unproductive expenditure of time and resources.

Engaging In Ether Mining On The Ethereum Platform

There is no obligation for you to purchase ether if you do not desire to do so. One can engage in the process of mining to obtain it, and the following is a detailed explanation of the procedure.

Please install the C visual component on your computer.

You will be tasked with operating either a computer utilizing a 64-bit architecture or one running on a 32-bit architecture. When downloading C to mine effectively, it will be necessary to obtain the appropriate visual from Microsoft. If feasible, it is advisable to utilize a 64-bit computer for mining ether, as the 32-bit system presents certain deficiencies in this regard. However, in the event that is the sole resource at your disposal, you must exercise patience with the program as it endeavours to resolve its shortcomings.

Install ethereum

The subsequent action entails the retrieval of Mist through downloading. Mist is a sophisticated graphical user interface (GUI) that will serve as the dedicated platform for managing your ethereum wallet. Mist possesses a user-oriented interface and provides assistance via a browser-based application that you would be inclined to acquire, thereby enabling you to connect with individuals capable of offering aid whenever necessary.

Get blockchain

This process will require a considerable amount of time on your part, as it involves the downloading of the complete blockchain onto your computer. The file that you are about to download is a file with a size of ten gigabytes. Therefore, it is advisable to engage in alternative activities during the course of downloading this file.

Establish your financial account

Now would be an opportune moment for you to establish your wallet. There is a multitude of options available to you when it comes to selecting which wallet to utilize. In order to make an informed decision, it is imperative to assess the security features inherent to the wallet, along with the advantages that accrue from employing said wallet, ultimately determining the optimal choice for personal utilization. Possessing a wallet is of utmost importance as it serves as the designated repository for the allocation of your ether earnings resulting from your diligent efforts.

Install the Nvidia Cuda toolkit, the OpenCL Software Development Kit (SDK), or the AMD software suite.

Prior to installing the program that relies on the GPU, it is necessary to verify the compatibility and functionality of your GPU. The downloadable application will be tailored to the capabilities of your GPU.

Proceed with the installation of the AlethOne Miner.

It is highly probable that you are functioning as an independent worker, thus it would be advisable for you to acquire the AletheOne software by means of downloading it. AletheOne is the system on which you are currently engaged in mining activities. Please bear in mind that utilizing a 32-bit system for mining may result in system freezing and other complications, therefore it is advisable to steer clear of such systems.

Please await the initialization of the Directed Acyclic Graph (DAG).

Once AletheOne has completed its process, there will be a brief period of approximately ten minutes during which you will need to wait in order to construct a Directed Acyclic Graph (DAG). The DAG file will be retained in the Random Access Memory (RAM) of the computers, in order to develop an algorithm that effectively safeguards against Application-Specific Integrated Circuit (ASIC) capabilities.

Participate in a mining consortium

It is quite unlikely that one would secure a job in a warehouse abundant with GPUs. Hence, it would be prudent to seek out a mining pool that aligns well with your specific requirements. This will revert to the competition that was previously mentioned in your reading material. It is advisable not to associate oneself with a mining pool that exhibits a substantial number of miners, as it would result in an arduous competition. This can occur when there are individuals who possess greater proficiency than oneself. By placing oneself in such a situation, there is a possibility of not receiving due recognition for one's efforts.

Alternatively, if recognition is indeed bestowed, it may not reach its full potential in terms of magnitude.